TRIUMPH IN SUFFERING.

A DISCOURSE

DELIVERED AT THE

FUNERAL OF THE REV. I. S. SPENCER, D.D.,

PASTOR OF THE

SECOND PRESBYTERIAN CHURCH IN BROOKLYN, L. I.

BY

GARDINER SPRING, D.D., L.L.D.,

Pastor of the Brick Presbyterian Church in the City of New York.

NEW YORK:

M. W. DODD, PUBLISHER,

BRICK CHURCH CHAPEL, CITY HALL SQUARE.

1855.

TRIUMPH IN SUFFERING.

A DISCOURSE

DELIVERED AT THE

FUNERAL OF THE REV. I. S. SPENCER, D.D.,

PASTOR OF THE

SECOND PRESBYTERIAN CHURCH IN BROOKLYN, L. I.

BY

GARDINER SPRING, D.D., L.L.D.,

Pastor of the Brick Presbyterian Church in the City of New York.

NEW YORK:

M. W. DODD, PUBLISHER,

BRICK CHURCH CHAPEL, CITY HALL SQUARE.

1855.

TRIUMPH IN SUFFERING.

"FOR I RECKON THAT THE SUFFERINGS OF THIS PRESENT TIME ARE NOT WORTHY TO BE COMPARED WITH THE GLORY WHICH SHALL BE REVEALED IN US."—ROMANS viii. 18.

NOTWITHSTANDING the excellencies of his personal and official character, the strong and lurid light in which our departed brother is presented to my own thoughts, is his *triumph in suffering.* The cross and the crown—present suffering and the future glory—are fitting themes on this mournful occasion. There is nothing in Christianity, nor in the character of Christians, nor in the relation they sustain to the Church or the world, that exempts them from present suffering. Whoever reads the Epistles addressed to the early Christians, will be convinced that, so far from being exempted from this allotment, *their* trials were such as have rarely been surpassed. They were set forth as "spectacles" of suffering, in order to show what living Christianity is, what it can endure, and how it shines in the hottest furnace. In the strong language of Paul, "They were always delivered unto death for Jesus' sake, that the life, also, of Jesus might be made manifest in their mortal flesh." But they had consolations to which other men were strangers. Pain and agony, chains and the dungeon, hungry lions and fierce flames could not disturb the thinking, tranquil, joyful, triumphant spirit; it scarcely sympathized with these torturing agonies, except in its struggles to be free. The darkest night of tribulation did not obscure the light of God's countenance; nor did its deepest depths shut out the comforting and vivid anticipations of the incorruptible, undefiled, and unfading inheritance. In view of this inheritance, all that earth could inflict was not worthy of a thought. "I reckon," exclaims that suffering and triumphant apostle, "that the sufferings of this present time are *not worthy to be compared* with the glory which shall be revealed in us."

Yet many are the persons, and many is the time when they are so compared, and when Christian men are so absorbed in the contemplation of them, and so studious of deliverance from them, as to lose sight of the attractions of their high and glorious inheritance.

We may find instruction, therefore, in so arranging our thoughts as to show—

How present sufferings are *thus compared* with the future glory;

And *how unwise it is* to suffer them to be thus brought into competition.

I. We are, in the first place, to show *how present sufferings are thus compared with the future glory.*

If good men were not exposed to set their affections on the things of earth and time, there would have been no occasion for those oft-repeated and urgent admonitions against a worldly spirit, which meet us in almost every page of the sacred writings. The tendency towards earth is strong, even in the regenerated mind. Transient and unsatisfying as they are, the affections linger about "these mortal shores." Nor is it always merely for the positive good which the things of earth will confer; but to secure exemption from trials, to avoid the mortification of an humble and depressed condition, and escape the embarrassment and trials which the absence of worldly good inflicts. When, in seasons of spiritual degeneracy, we magnify perplexing cares and disheartening disappointments, and contemplate the evils of the present life as the greatest object of our aversion; and when, to alleviate them, we set our hearts on the pursuit or possession of worldly good, we take a very disproportionate and wrong view of the present and the future. This undue fear of trials, and this excessive love of earth, depreciate the glory of the heavenly kingdom. Whoever yields to it allows time to usurp the place of eternity, earth the place of heaven, and the sorrows of earth the place of boundless and eternal joys. He compares the "vapor that appeareth for a little time and then vanisheth away," with the bliss which eternity only can measure or comprehend.

The religion that shines brightly in prosperity is very apt to shine in adversity. There is a buoyancy of heart in trials, a joy in tribulation, which indicates that the sufferer is conscious that here he has no abiding city, and is looking for one which "hath foundations, whose builder and maker is God." This earth presents no nobler view than struggling poverty cheered by the promise of durable riches; undeserved reproach comforted with the assurance of everlasting honors; and a mind supported, peaceful and happy, in a body withered by disease and bleeding under the pangs of unalleviated pain. Such a sufferer confers abundant honor on the "word on which God has caused him to hope," and on the great realities of the coming world. But when trials oppress the heart, and good men allow themselves to be weighed down with the burden, and sink in uncontrollable sadness, they not only do injustice to themselves, but to their promised inheritance. They dwell so much, and with so much discouragement, upon their sufferings, and look so intensely upon the goblet that contains the wormwood and the gall, that they tempt the tempter, and lay their own minds open to that dark and morbid melancholy which unfits them alike for duty and enjoyment. They even lose their relish for the truths and privileges which the Gospel imparts, and instead of finding comfort in the anticipation of what awaits them beyond this world, look with doubt and suspicion upon the full cup of blessing which infinite love would fain put to their lips. A moderated and submissive grief is one of the best proofs that the divine discipline is producing its desired effect. But this is a very different thing from that inexorable despondency in which the soul "*refuses* to be comforted." What is more apparent, when this is the case, than that the sufferer has forgotten that there is a better world, and depreciates the glories of those "sweet fields beyond the flood?" How light would trials appear compared with the glory to be revealed, if that "exceeding and eternal weight of glory" could be seen without a cloud! How would the darkest sky drop with mercy, and the breeze of the pestilence become fragrant, and the habitations of woe, and the place of sighing become vocal with joy and praise, if our hearts and hopes were always and more sensibly lodged in heaven! Oh! they are delighted visions, hallowed, transforming, transporting views, when the soul realizes them, and lingers amid such scenes, and feels that every rough wind that blows, and every dark wave and adverse current, is drifting it to the heavenly shore. The heir apparent of an earthly kingdom may meet with crosses and disappointments, conflicts and temporary defeat; but the power, and wealth, and honor that await him when he shall grasp the sceptre and assume the diadem, make him ashamed to indulge in sadness which might be befitting those of more humble expectations. And what shall be said of those who are to receive the crown of righteousness, and reign in life with Christ, when they give way to a spirit of immoderate and uncontrolled sorrow, but that they allow the sufferings of this present time to compare with, if not for a season to supersede, the glory to be revealed?

When the heart is thus oppressed with trials, there are also strong inducements *to sin*, in order to *avoid trials*. Men sin, not only for the positive enjoyment which sin furnishes them as creatures of sense, but for the negative enjoyment of avoiding the ills which flesh and sense are heirs to. Not a few of the trials which befall men are the consequence of an inflexible adherence to duty. Paul was a sufferer because he was a Christian. The martyrs were sufferers because they would not throw a handful of incense on the altars of idolatry. And thousands have trodden in their steps, and followed their upward path to the glory from which all the sufferings of time could not wean them. No man knows the strength of his piety until he is tried. Not unfrequently we may, and no doubt often do, avoid embarrassment and difficulty, by aberrations from moral rectitude, and indifference to the claims of truth and righteousness. Poverty may be avoided by the accumulation of unrighteous gains; obscurity may be avoided by those who will hesitate at nothing in their pursuit of dignity and place; punishment and disgrace may be avoided by falsehood, and we may screen others from them if we are willing to do it at the expense of our integrity. Men may retain the favor of their fellow-men, and extend the circle of their friends and influence, if they will connive at the wickedness of the rich, and minister to the vices of the poor. Ministers of the Gospel may attain the popularity they seek after, by "preaching smooth things, prophesying deceits," and saying, "Peace, peace," when God says "there is no peace to the wicked." Various are the ways in which temporary evil may be avoided, and temporary good secured *by the sacrifice of principle.* But in no instance can this be done without a manifest preference of exemption from present trial, to the "favor which the Lord bears to his own people." Let every man who had rather sin than suffer, faithfully inspect the actings of his own mind, and his own inward questionings will show him that in every such preference he is not only comparing the afflictions of time with everlasting glory, but actually deciding in favor of the earthly and against the heavenly.

Not unfrequently, also, *the gracious design of affliction is lost sight of.* The proper fruit of present suffering is to take away sin, and fit the soul for heaven. He who sends it "does not afflict willingly, nor grieve the children of men;" the end is unutterably desirable, and may well reconcile the severest sufferer to his sharpest pangs. "My brethren," says the apostle James, "count it all joy when ye fall into divers trials, knowing this, that the trial of your faith worketh patience; but let patience have her *perfect* work, that ye may be perfect and entire, wanting nothing." Yet how often are the people of God most grieved when they have the most cause to live upon the promises, and to count upon their spiritual and eternal joys! With thoughts more employed about their present troubles than the end towards which they are conducting them, they forget that "God has chosen them in the furnace of affliction," and that whom the Lord "loveth he chasteneth, and scourgeth every son whom he receiveth." Instead of appreciating the truth that "it is through much tribulation they must enter the kingdom," they not only repine at their trials, but overlook their certain and blessed issue. This seems very much like comparing heaven with present exemption from sorrow, and balancing them as rival claims.

There are also *instances, not a few, in which the soul is lost by its solicitude to avoid present suffering.* Good men may sin in order to avoid suffering, and because they have seen their folly, repented of their wickedness, and apprehended the mercy of God in Christ, will be saved from the penal consequences of the guilty choice, and find pardon and life. But it is far otherwise with those who persevere in their sinful courses, and, rather than be sufferers, throw away their immortality. Unlike him who "chose rather to suffer affliction with the people of God than to enjoy the pleasures of sin for a season," they will not part with the pleasures of sin, even for the glory which is to be revealed. It is not the purity of heaven that attracts them, but the pollutions of earth. They will not "break loose from this enchanted ground," though it were for the splendor and blessedness of the Celestial City. They choose rather "to *have* their sins and go to hell, than to *leave* their sins and go to heaven." Consult their desires for the present world, and they forego every other hope and rush upon destruction. This is the spirit that governs them. It is the death of seriousness, and drowns them in destruction and perdition.

No Christian does this. In his view there is no room for the comparison between the present and the future. All the pleasures he can enjoy in the present world, and all the sufferings he can endure, are not worthy of a second thought, if suffered to detract from the purity or elevation of his character, or obscure the glory of his final inheritance. Paul so reckoned; and there are good reasons for this conclusion. Let us, then,—

II. In the second place, suggest some of the reasons which indicate the folly of allowing present suffering and future glory to be thus brought into competition.

We must here limit ourselves to the three following thoughts:

1. In the first place, present sufferings *may be endured.*

We speak not lightly of present sufferings; "we remember the wormwood and the gall, and our flesh trembleth at God's judgments." Yet in all their multitude and varied degrees of severity, they have been endured, and can be endured still. Poverty may be endured, though it reduce a man to the bread and water of affliction, and clothe him with rags, and fierce winds whistle through his shattered dwelling. Shame and reproach may be endured, and though they drive the sufferer into solitude, they must prey long upon him before his unbending spirit is crushed. Persecution may inflict its terrors, and chase its victims into dens and caves of the earth, and they may yet live, and be contented and happy. Sickness may debilitate, and the bed of languishing may be the bed of peace. Pain may agonize this curiously-framed machinery, and if it do not dart its pangs through some vital organ, the machinery will last, and be sustained under weeks, and months, and years of suffering. The great Creator has so formed these bodies, and so fenced round the seat of life with bones and sinews, that the citadel is able to withstand many a severe and stormy siege before it yields to the King of Terrors. The waste of human life is a gradual process; and its resuscitating power for a long time stands abreast with its decay. The history of human suffering would be a most touching history, but it would be the narrative of almost incredible *endurance.* It is not wonderful that men should exclaim with Job, "I would not live always;" while, at the same time, they *live* under untold complications of suffering and calamity. Instances are not wanting in which the mind, absorbed in other and more important and higher themes, forgets the sufferings of the body, and leaves its inferior companion to suffer forgotten and alone. There are noble examples of suffering on record, which seem to have been permitted in order to show that there are laws of God's providence, and higher laws of His truth and grace in Jesus Christ, by which the mind can triumph over the sufferings of the body, and demonstrate to what extent the immaterial possesses the mastery over the material.

We should probably be surprised to know to what extent these frail tenements of clay can be filled with pain and anguish, before "the silver cord" that binds them together is loosed. Not unfrequently has the conflict been prolonged for years, which, at the first onset, did not seem able to be endured for a day. Few, even of the men of the world, have ever been so overwhelmed with calamity as to be impatient for the relief which death only can give. And when the rare instance occurs, that the child of suffering and despair "chooses strangling and death, rather than life," how does the general surprise testify to the folly of the sentiment, that the sufferings of earth are too heavy to be borne. And where human endurance, and philosophy, lending her aid to native strength of mind, refuses an adequate support under sufferings, there are higher powers to support the sufferer than the powers of earth. Because the eternal God is his refuge and underneath him are the everlasting arms, his sufferings can be endured. Scenes of suffering there are where the Comforter never comes, no angel-forms hover, and where His voice is never heard who brought life and immortality to light. There is no vigor of intellect in that world of darkness, no strength of resolution, and no cold philosophy that can endure the loss of heaven and the soul. The man who has become a castaway may sit down and weep, and suffer his heart to break. He has no strong tower into which he may run and be safe, and no chamber of mercy where he may hide until the calamity be overpast. There is no revealed glory in those dark domains of perfect and absolute despair. Who, then, that knows the Christian's spirit and the Christian's hopes, will not judge with Paul, that present sufferings are not worthy to be compared with the future glory?

2. In the second place, the sufferings of this present time *may be mitigated.*

Few earthly trials are so great as to be incapable of alleviation. Be they what they may, the cup is never so full but many a drop of bitterness may be added to it before it overflows. There is much remaining to the most abject sufferer the sun looks upon, of which no suffering has yet deprived him. The great mass of sufferers, when they compare their own privations and sorrows with others, can always find those whose condition is more pitiable than their own. There are *comforts*, too, in the allotment of the afflicted, even when dwelling upon their darkest prospects; God "hath set one over against the other," so that no condition is one of unmingled evil. The sympathy of friends, the remembrance of the past, and the hope of the future—blessings unthought of in more prosperous days—the comparison of our sufferings with our ill desert, and the reflection that any thing short of being banished from heaven and shut up in hell, is more than we can claim at the hands of justice—all these come over the sufferer's mind like cooling showers upon the scorched and burning desert. To a Christian mind there is also the alleviating thought, that there is infinite wisdom and goodness in all his sufferings; that in covenanted mercy and faithfulness, all things work together for his good; and that this dark night is to be succeeded by a sun that never goes down. Nor is this all that alleviates his woes. There is one Comforter whose presence he enjoys, whom the men of the world know not. And He was a sufferer—the great, the Omnipotent Sufferer. We may not speak of our light and alleviated sufferings, when we think of His. Fearful wrath broke upon that guiltless head, when He hung on Calvary, and terrors gleamed there, compared with which the lightning that flashed on Sinai grows pale. That cross—that crown of thorns—that hammer and those nails—that uncovered body—that bitter cup—that furious and mocking soldiery—that hour and those powers of darkness, waging their last and most terrific warfare, where no earthly friend may comfort Him—no angel of all those legions come for His rescue, but He must sink and die alone, because Heaven is angry, and because He who is dearest to Him on earth and in heaven, hides His face — these were sufferings at which the heavens grew dark, and the vale of the temple was rent in twain, from the top to the bottom. No, we may not speak of our light and alleviated sufferings, when compared with His. Say, Christian sufferer, is there nothing in that cross that binds up thy broken and sustains thy sinking heart. Does that bleeding One never wipe the sorrows from thy cheek? We have seen the subjects of sorrow, and have been conversant with chambers where none could refrain from weeping but the sufferer, and where he, of all the others, was the most comforted, because "the Man of Sorrows" was his Comforter. Has that great and triumphant Sufferer given no promises to his suffering people, that "His grace shall be sufficient for them," and that they shall be the happier for every tear they shed? Have burning martyrs never sung and shouted amid the ascending flames, because there was One in the furnace with them like "unto the Son of Man?" Oh! could we go to yonder hospital, or stand by the ten thousand beds of suffering with which this poor world is filled, how many thousands should we see, who, from the lowest depths of suffering, climb the highest altitude of hope and joy and heavenly anticipation to which faith can soar! Every Christian grace brought into exercise, and burnished by sufferings, does itself soothe and staunch the bleeding heart. That widow's heart which is buried in her husband's grave, has a sacred calmness, because she has learned to say, "It is the Lord, let him do what seemeth him good." That suffering man of God has mitigations of his sufferings, which we might well consent to endure, if we could but enjoy them. His weather-beaten bark labors and plunges in the tempest, but all around him are the circling hills of the New Jerusalem. Shame on the Christian who, amid such teachings and such assurances of the Saviour's love, stoops to put present sufferings in competition with the coming glory!

But what can soothe under eternal losses? Or who shall suggest an availing consolation to him who is an outcast from the kingdom of God? The loss is complete; the woe is finished, entire, and unmitigated. No voice of compassion, no remembrance of the past, no hope of the future, no bland graces of the Spirit buoy up the burdened heart. No ray of light comes into the dark dungeon. In all the wide universe there is no being, nor object, nor thought, nor emotion, that brings sympathy or succor. Evil, merited, intolerable, unmitigated, and unrelieved, must be the portion of such a sufferer. And who, much more what Christian, can for a moment put in competition present sufferings, not with the future glory merely, but with these irreparable evils? I add,—

3. In the third place, and it is a delightful thought, that the sufferings of this life *have an end.*

To indicate their brevity, they are called "the sufferings of *this present time*," and "light afflictions which endure *but for a moment.*" More usually, if not always, they admit of variations; the man whose sky has been overcast, and whose courage has drooped in the storm, has often, unexpectedly, found the clouds clear away, and the smile of Heaven resting upon his head. But even where trials can no longer be mitigated nor endured, they last but a little while. It is a terrible struggle; but, blessed be God who made man's life what it is, flesh and sense at length give way, and then all his troubles are "as a dream when one awaketh." When they "have killed the body," they have done their worst; after that, they have no more that they can do. "The wind passeth over them, and they are gone, and the place thereof knoweth them no more." When the Christian lies down in the grave, want ceases to assail him; suspicion and obloquy and neglect no longer mortify him; separations no longer break his heart; crosses and disappointments no longer interrupt his peace; pain, and groans, and "dying strife" no longer agonize his poor, suffering body. This final catastrophe ends the history of his trials. You heard it, you saw it, but it was the last groan, the last throb of anguish, the last tear he will ever shed. The conflict is over. There will be no more exhausting days and wearisome nights. The aching head, the throbbing heart, are at rest. Adversity has spent the last arrow in his quiver, and the child of sorrow has found his final and perfect repose.

But the glory that "is to be revealed" is but just begun. Just as "the wrath to come" remains "the wrath to come," and still "to come;" so the "glory that is to be revealed" remains the glory to be yet revealed, and in progressive and augmented revelations for interminable ages. As "he that is filthy shall be filthy still," so "he that is holy shall be holy still." These chilling winds and changing seasons are there unknown. The soul that once enters that happy world is for ever out of their reach. Throughout all the bright regions of that New Creation, there are songs and everlasting joy upon their heads, and the splendors of everlasting day. Crowns such as angels wear are there, and a throne of glory where they shall live and reign with Christ for ever. Oh! do not the sufferings of this present time actually vanish before this unspeakable glory? May they be brought into comparison? Shall the shadow of time obscure the lustre of eternity?

What strange blindness, what madness even, is in the human heart? Who but a creature fallen by his iniquity, would ever have thought of thus putting in competition such things as these? What moral arithmetic is this, and where is it taught and learned?

Who is the teacher of this great delusion but the "father of lies?" Yet our poor, infatuated earth is full of it. Sometimes, as we survey it, it looks to us as a great madhouse, where "the god of this world hath blinded the minds of them that believe not, lest the light of the glorious Gospel should shine unto them." We see for ourselves that "even the mind and conscience" are defiled by sin. If men reasoned in other matters as they do on the subject of religion, and formed their estimate by the same obscured vision by which they allow the present to come in competition with the future, we might justly consider them maniacs. My bereaved hearers who have no hope, and are without God in the world, you may not look for exemption from trials. Your dwellings, and your own bosoms, will yet give forth the echo to many a sad tale of woe. And what if you have nothing beyond the present to hope for? Oh! the stupidity, the amazing temerity of encountering the ills of human life, with no refuge from the storm! "*Madness* is in their heart while they live, and after that they go to the dead."

All are not thus reckless. Multitudes there are now in heaven, and even in this age of worldliness some there are yet remaining on the earth, who lay their account with trial and suffering; who are satisfied that "it is through much tribulation they must enter into the kingdom;" and who are happy in the thought that "it worketh out for them a far more exceeding and eternal weight of glory." They are comforted in their sufferings, and are often cheerful and happy under the heaviest frowns. All of joy and woe which this world contains is to them but dust in the balance to the glorious realities that remain.

The beloved man whose untimely death we all so

deeply deplore, was a sufferer; but he was not guilty of the folly of "comparing the sufferings of this present time with the glory that shall be revealed." His affections were not set on the things of earth and time; nor did he allow them to come in competition with the favors of his Divine Master. The Church of God has not many such ministers of the Gospel to lose as Dr. Spencer. His brethren in the ministry have rarely, if ever, been called to mourn a heavier loss. This is an affecting scene, my hearers, to him who now addresses you, as well as to yourselves. There lies the man who I fondly hoped would live to preach my funeral sermon. Yet, though endowed with a more vigorous frame, though in the high day of unwearied toil and usefulness, and though more than half a score of years behind me, he is the first to reach the goal, and gain the prize. I have never felt more deeply than I now do, that with all its distinguished blessings, one of the penalties of long life is, that we live to see so many others die.

The early history of our departed brother was not unlike that of many of his brethren in the sacred calling, and not a few of eminence in other professions in our youthful land. Under God's guidance and blessing, he was a *self-made* man. *Ichabod Smith Spencer* was born of Christian parents, in the town of Rupert, Bennington County, in the State of Vermont, February 3, 1797. His father, one of two brothers, was a respected agriculturist, that could do little more for his children than furnish them with those rudiments of education which are so well supplied by the common schools of New-England. This son was the child of many prayers, faithful and kind discipline, and assiduous religious culture. He became hopefully pious in his youth, and at an early age united himself with the church of God. At seventeen years of age he was thrown upon his own resources; and with no pecuniary assistance except that which he derived from his emoluments as a teacher, was fitted for college at the Academy in Salem, in the State of New York. Here it was his privilege to enjoy the friendship and paternal counsels of that venerable and beloved man, whose praise is in all the churches, the Rev. Alexander Proudfit, whom he never ceased to regard with filial affection. At Union College he maintained a high standing in his class, and was graduated with honor in the year 1822. He was immediately employed as a teacher in the grammar-school in Schenectady, and with his eye and heart on the pulpit, at the same time pursued his theological studies under the direction of the Rev. Dr. Yates, the Professor of Moral Philosophy in the College. He subsequently became the Preceptor of the Academy in Canandaigua, where he so far completed his theological studies, as to receive his licensure to preach the Gospel.

Though, as he himself has often remarked, his preparations for the ministry were far from being ample; unwearied diligence, a well-disciplined mind, and a character of great decision and loveliness, soon convinced the churches that he was no common man, and prepared the way for his occupying one of the most important pulpits in New England. He was the worthy successor of Stoddard, Edwards, and Williams, and an able defender of the truths of the Gospel, at a time when so many of the churches of New England had departed from the faith of their Puritan ancestors. Long will he be remembered in Northampton; where, though his ministry was continued but three and a-half years, it was attended with great success. His occasional visits to that people, after the dissolution of his pastoral charge, were hailed with every token of Christian affection on the part of the people, and greatly enjoyed by himself. He left Northampton for Brooklyn in 1832, to take the charge of this then infant and newly-organized church, where he continued in the pastoral office until his death, the 23d of November, 1854, at the age of nearly 57 years.

I need not inform this church and congregation what he was as a man, a minister of the Gospel, and a pastor. He has left his impress upon this people, nor will it be easy to erase it. He sought not yours, but you. There are seals of his ministry here, which show what manner of man he was in the midst of you. The signs of a faithful minister have been wrought among you in all patience and mighty deeds. Ye are his epistles, known and read of all men. Ye are his witnesses that " by the word of truth, by the power of God, by the armor of righteousness on the right hand and on the left, by pureness, by knowledge, by long-suffering, by kindness, by the Holy Ghost, by love unfeigned," he " approved himself as the minister of God."

It is characteristic of the best ministers that they are best at home, and most distinguished in their own pulpits. There was no " flourish of trumpets" with Dr. Spencer, when he went abroad. He was not demonstrative in his nature, nor eager for the praise of men. He was emulous, but it was mainly to magnify the truths of God, and do good to the souls of men. No man was less desirous than he to " create a sensation," and set the world aghast by his preaching. Yet was he exclusively devoted to his work. His heart, his thoughts, his studies and attainments, his time, his interests, his influence, and his life, were given to the ministry. Few ministers of the everlasting Gospel, if any, are more industrious; and few have less occasion to lament misspent and wasted hours. The result was, that he became one of the best and most effective preachers of the age. Few habitually spake like him in discourses of such instructiveness, such attractive persuasion, such withering rebuke of wickedness, or such happy effects upon the minds of men. He "spake the things which become sound doctrine," and declared "the whole counsel of God." He was cautious and wise, but he was urgent and in earnest. He was often tender to weeping, yet was he a most fearless preacher. There was a large commingling of the "Son of consolation" with the "Son of thunder" in his character. I have heard him say that he *did not know what it was to be ensnared or embarrassed in preaching God's truth, and that the thought of being afraid to utter it because it was unpopular, never once entered his mind.* There was something of nature in this, and more of grace; he was fearless of men, because he feared God. There was great variety in his preaching; he was not confined to a few threadbare topics; his mind and heart took a wide range, and brought out of his treasure "things both new and old." Nor was he given to crude and imperfect preparations for the pulpit; a volume of sermons might be selected from his manuscripts, which would be a beautiful model for the youthful ministry, and a great comfort to the Church of God. His Sabbath evening lectures on the Shorter Catechism, as well as portions of his lectures on the Epistle to the Romans, will not easily be forgotten by those who heard them.

In his style of writing, and in his style and manner of

preaching, he was manly, strong, and energetic, rather than rhetorical. His thoughts were weighty, his imagination rich; but they were sweet thoughts, and hallowed imaginations. He had no verbiage. I know no man whose piety and taste more instinctively revolted from the ostentation of words; his words were simple and "fitly spoken," and his style remarkably terse and sententious. There was now and then an iron nerve about his discourses and manner, and a flash of thought that were startling, and that broke upon his hearers like a voice of thunder. Yet with all this startling boldness, there was sweetness, humility, and meekness, and those deep and realizing views of divine truth which indicated that he was taught of God. It was not difficult to perceive that he was no stranger to the duties of the closet. In his own pulpit, his *prayers* were distinguished, not only for their devotional spirit, but for their appropriateness and variety. Those who have heard him most, and longest, and most attentively, have remarked that they never knew any thing like repetition in his prayers, and never enjoyed such variety of sacred thought and emotion as they enjoyed from his devotional exercises.

He excelled also as a *pastor*. His parochial duties were his labor and delight. There was great faithfulness, great painstaking, and even great *tact* in his pastoral services. The life of a pastor consists, in no small degree, in the study of personal character, and in the study and exhibition of those divine truths that are adapted to the character and experience of those committed to his charge. Dr. Spencer's "Pastoral Sketches," a work of great interest in itself, and great value to ministers, and to all inquiring minds, illustrates his great excellence in this department of ministerial labor. Would that we were all more like him, in marking and in treasuring up the actings of the human heart, in watching the progress of serious thought, in following the leadings of the Divine Spirit upon the minds of our people, and in addressing to them the right truth, in the right way, and at the right time! His acquaintance with the spiritual history of his people gave him prodigious advantage over their minds in his discourses from the pulpit. His portraits of character were to the life, and though they were delicately drawn, and without personal allusion, there was no escape from the grasp of truth when he put the screws upon the conscience, and made the law and the Gospel alike utter the words of Nathan to David, "Thou art the man." And the beauty of the process was, that he did it with a tenderness and *sympathy* that so linked the speaker with the hearers, that the stout-hearted could not complain, and the broken-hearted were made whole. He had no theory of "revivals," yet was he often in the midst of them. God's truth, God's Spirit, and the prayers of his people, were the only agencies he relied on, and he found them abundantly adequate to their end. God gave him souls for his hire. This is the reward he sought after, and he enjoys it now.

I need not speak of *his life*. He is the only man who ever doubted that he was a man of genuine piety. "Whatsoever things are true, whatsoever things are honest, whatsoever things are just, whatsoever things are pure, whatsoever things are lovely, whatsoever things are of good report; if there be any virtue, and if there be any praise," these things belonged to Dr. Spencer. Not a blot rests upon his fair name. The perplexed will miss his counsels, the afflicted will miss his sympathy, and the poor of Brooklyn will miss his laborious charities.

I have said more than once that he was a *sufferer.* Nor may I close without asking you to go with me to his chamber of suffering and triumph. "It is better to go to the house of mourning than to the house of feasting." Beyond the banqueting-halls of the rich and the palaces of princes, is the "chamber where the good man meets his fate." His voice will not be soon forgotten as uttered from the pulpit; "but being dead he yet speaketh" from that sad and triumphant chamber. He was a sufferer for years, and his sufferings sometimes oppressed his heart, because they unfitted him for active labor; yet I have seen him more depressed when the sunlight of prosperity shone upon him, than in the dark night of his affliction. His graces grew under the sharpest trials; and amid all the outward darkness with which he was so long enveloped, his path shone brighter and brighter unto the perfect day.

During the last three or four weeks of his life, so severe were his sufferings, that he was not inclined to much conversation. But on the Monday preceding his death, being comparatively free from pain, and perceiving that his time was short, he called his family about his bed, requested them to be so arranged that he could see them all, and separately address each one of them. He told them that he expected to die, and expected to go to heaven, and expressed the hope that he should meet them all there. In his own simple manner, and with all the tenderness of a dying man, he opened to them the way of life by Jesus Christ, spoke to them of his own confidence in the Saviour, and urged them to "cling to Christ and the Bible" as their only hope.

It was just after this affecting scene, that I knocked at

his door. And never was I more kindly directed than in making this fraternal visit. I had some fears, from what I knew of his self-scrutinizing spirit, that I might find him in a depressed state of mind. But as he drew near the close of his struggles, God was kind, and gave him sweet indications of his paternal love. There he tossed, day after day, and night after night, upon that couch of racking pain, with a mind as clear as Newton's, and a heart as peaceful as a child in its mother's bosom. The great peculiarity of his Christian character was his shrinking humility and self-diffidence. More than once, in the days of his unbroken vigor, I have heard him say, "I have mistaken my calling; I never was fit for a minister of the Gospel." No one else thought so; yet he retained this self-diffidence to the last. I said to him, "Brother Spencer, I am afraid you are about to leave us." He replied, "I think so." I took his hand, and he said, "You see I am strong; I may rally, but it is more than probable that I shall leave you by to-morrow morning." "Is it *peace* with you, brother?" His body was in agony; he tossed his head on the pillow, and replied, "*It is all peace!*" He paused, and, fixing his piercing eye upon me, said, "I am afraid *it is too much peace.* I cannot discover in myself those evidences of personal godliness which justify me in enjoying *such abundant peace.*" I could not repress a smile at these sweet words, and then reminded him of those words of the Lord Jesus, when He said, "I am come that they might have life, and that they might have it *more abundantly.*" He simply replied, "Pray with me;" and then called his family around his bed, where we knelt and prayed together for the last time. His sufferings continued without any abatement, with the exception of a few tranquil hours, which he employed in giving to those around him his last counsels and charge, commending them to God, and testifying his own precious hopes, and the prospects that cheered him as he bade them farewell. He subsequently conversed but little. His manly frame was exhausted. Three days after this the strong man bowed himself to the impotence and dust of death. An inscrutable Providence made him a partaker in his Master's sufferings; abundant grace made him partaker in His glory.

"God's way is in the sea, and His path in the mighty waters, and His footsteps are not known." It is a dark day in which we live. There is a fearful dying of God's faithful ministers and people, as though He would take them away from the evil that is coming on the land, on the Church, and on the world, and hide them in His own pavilion. It is a dark day to a loving and bereaved family and congregation, when such a husband, such a father, such a pastor, is summoned from earth to heaven. It is a dark day to Brooklyn, when, amid bold and unchecked errors, a man of such firm principles, and conservative, equable spirit, is removed from so commanding a pulpit. It is a dark day to *us*, his brethren in the ministry, when a light that burned so brightly, and which we had hoped would burn so long, is put out. He who addresses you has been permitted to live while two generations of ministers have dropped around him into the grave. We adore God's goodness, while we still feel that His ways are dark, and that He is speaking to us in His voice of storms. We are dumb with silence, and can only look round for some refuge in this day of trouble.

My brethren in the ministry, and my friends of this mourning congregation, "God is a refuge for us."

O ye, the most beloved and most bereaved! if ye would see brother Spencer, ye must not look to that dissolving tabernacle. It is taken down, and he is not there. I would not have him return to it, and again pass through those scenes of agony! No, the conflict is over. Brother! brother! all hail! The conflict is over, and the victory is won! What does *he* think of his sufferings *now*, and of the storms that have blown him into such a harbor? Oh! we would fain climb these cliffs of time, and with him take a view of the world of joy. There the children of adversity are made free from sorrow. There are those "who came out of great tribulation, having washed their robes and made them white in the blood of the Lamb." There the exiled is an heir of God, and a joint-heir with Jesus Christ. There the captive gains the prize and wears the crown. There there is nothing that defileth. There every devout emotion is gratified, every thought glows with rapture, every joy is unspeakable and full of glory. There the "Lamb which is in the midst of the throne shall feed them, and lead them to living fountains of water. They shall hunger no more, neither thirst any more, neither shall the sun light on them, nor any heat." There "God shall wipe away all tears from their eyes: there shall be no more *death*, neither *sorrow*, neither *crying*, neither shall there be *any more pain;* for the former things are passed away." As certainly as "the Son of Man came to seek and to save that which is lost," so certainly our beloved and departed brother is there. The Gospel is triumphant in the life and death of such a man, and it is triumph in suffering. What a triumphant chamber was that! and what an hour of triumph when that creature of suffering, poor in spirit, but rich in faith and heavenly hopes, was released from the bondage in which he had so long struggled, dismissed from this sinning and weeping world, and winged his way to his appointed and prepared place near the eternal throne! "I am going," he exclaimed, "to a world where there is no sickness, no pain, no temptation, and no sin!" Language fails, thought is feeble, in the contemplation of such a scene. Angels stoop to look upon it, and wait to bear the liberated spirit away. Oh! what inexpressible glory bursts upon that ransomed spirit when, having dropped the burden of sin and woe, passed these confines of darkness and fear, and gained those realms of light, he is welcomed home!

Could he look to-day from those holy, happy scenes, upon *whom* would he look, and *what* would he say? He would look upon you who most deeply mourn, and say, "*Dry up those tears. Thy Maker is thy husband, and let thy fatherless children trust in Him.*" *This will give you security and comfort, even in this vale of tears. The widow's God and the Father of the fatherless will not disappoint the hopes that rest upon His promises!* He would look upon the church he has gathered, upon the old he has encouraged and comforted, and upon the young he has watched over, upon the poor he has ministered to, and the wandering he has gathered into the fold, and say, "*Be ye followers of them who through faith and patience have inherited the promises. We shall meet again, and let it be before that throne where your pastor would fain say, 'Behold I and the children which God hath given me!'*" He would cast his eye of Paternal love upon those who, with him, have served at God's altars, and say, "*Beloved brethren, walk circumspectly, not as fools, but as wise, redeeming the time. The glory to be revealed alone can estimate the immeasurable importance of your work. Take heed lest, after having preached to others, you yourselves be cast away. Your own salvation, and that of thousands, depends on your faithfulness. The day of retribution is near ; keep the faith, and finish your course with joy.*" He would look also with more than his wonted tenderness upon you who have long heard and long refused the salvation he proclaimed, and say, "*My beloved friends, I am no more in the midst of you. Many are the Sabbaths we have spent together in the world where I no longer dwell. Your consciences bear witness that I have employed those days of mercy in beseeching you to be reconciled to God. 'Remember the words that I spake to you, while I was yet with you,' and no longer despise this heavenly glory.*"

www.ingramcontent.com/pod-product-compliance
Lightning Source LLC
LaVergne TN
LVHW020741120826
845150LV00010B/2341

* 9 7 8 1 4 1 8 1 9 5 0 4 5 *